AXIS PARENT GUIDES SERIES

A Parent's Guide to the Sex Talk

A Parent's Guide to Pornography

A Parent's Guide to Sexual Assault

A Parent's Guide to Suicide & Self-Harm Prevention

A Parent's Guide to Depression & Anxiety

A Parent's Guide to Tough Conversations

A Parent's Guide to Cancel Culture

A Parent's Guide to Racism in the United States

A Parent's Guide to Walking through Grief

A Parent's Guide to Talking about Death

PARENT GUIDE BUNDLES

Parent Guides to Social Media

Parent Guides to Finding True Identity

Parent Guides to Mental & Sexual Health

Parent Guides to Connecting in Chaos

A PARENT'S GUIDE TO
TALKING ABOUT DEATH

A PARENT'S GUIDE TO

TALKING ABOUT DEATH

axis

Tyndale House Publishers
Carol Stream, Illinois

Visit Tyndale online at tyndale.com.

Visit Axis online at axis.org.

Tyndale and Tyndale's quill logo are registered trademarks of Tyndale House Ministries.

A Parent's Guide to Talking about Death

Designed by Lindsey Bergsma

Scripture quotations are taken from the Holy Bible, *New International Version,*® *NIV.*® Copyright © 1973, 1978, 1984, 2011 by Biblica, Inc.® Used by permission. All rights reserved worldwide.

For information about special discounts for bulk purchases, please contact Tyndale House Publishers at csresponse@tyndale.com, or call 1-855-277-9400.

Library of Congress Cataloging-in-Publication Data

A catalog record for this book is available from the Library of Congress.

ISBN 978-1-4964-6790-4

Printed in the United States of America

29	28	27	26	25	24	23
7	6	5	4	3	2	1

Most of us spend much time and energy trying to avoid the reality that we and those we love will die. But in facing the reality of death, we learn how to live rightly. We learn how to live in light of our limits and the brevity of our lives. And we learn to live in the hope of the resurrection.

LITURGY OF THE ORDINARY BY TISH HARRISON WARREN

CONTENTS

A LETTER FROM AXIS

Dear Reader,

We're Axis, and since 2007, we've been creating resources to help connect parents, teens, and Jesus in a disconnected world. We're a group of gospel-minded researchers, speakers, and content creators, and we're excited to bring you the best of what we've learned about making meaningful connections with the teens in your life.

This parent's guide is designed to help start a conversation. Our goal is to give you enough knowledge that you're able to ask your teen informed questions about their world. For each guide, we spend weeks reading, researching, and interviewing parents and teens in order to distill everything you need to know about the topic at hand. We encourage you to read the whole thing and then to use the questions we include to get the conversation going with your teen—and then to follow the conversation wherever it leads.

As Douglas Stone, Bruce Patton, and Sheila Heen point out in their book *Difficult Conversations*, "Changes in attitudes and behavior rarely come about because of arguments, facts, and attempts to persuade. How often do *you* change your values and beliefs—or whom you love or what you want in life—based on something someone tells you? And how likely are you to do so when the person who is trying to change you doesn't seem fully aware of the reasons you see things differently in the first place?"[1] For whatever reason, when we believe that others are trying to understand *our* point of view, our defenses usually go down, and we're more willing to listen to *their* point of view. The rising generation is no exception.

So we encourage you to ask questions, to listen, and then to share your heart with your teen. As we often say at Axis, discipleship happens where conversation happens.

Sincerely,
Your friends at Axis

---

[1] Douglas Stone, Bruce Patton, and Sheila Heen, *Difficult Conversations: How to Discuss What Matters Most*, rev. ed. (New York: Penguin Books, 2010), 137.

WHY SHOULD WE TALK ABOUT DEATH?

KNOWING HOW HEAVY and personal the topic of death can be, we want to start by saying thank you. Thank you for opening this guide. Thank you for choosing to walk with your teen, helping them process or prepare for their own encounters with death. Thank you for showing up for them, even as you might feel like you're breaking apart. We pray that the Father would meet you here, in this moment in time, in these pages—wherever you're coming from, whatever emotional state you find yourself in. We trust that He will give us what we need and be with us. Because of Jesus' righteousness, we can enter into God's loving presence.

Death has been called the ultimate statistic: ten out of every ten people will die. And although some professions come face-to-face with this reality on a more regular basis (doctors, nurses, police officers, military personnel), this conversation can be difficult to begin because much of American society is structured to keep the rest of us from thinking about death.

Since the 1800s, American culture has tried to "sanitize" death.[1] Bodies are embalmed to look more lifelike at funerals; loved ones often die in hospitals, not at home. When we do encounter death, our experience is often mediated by news outlets and screens.

> The dead often come to us by photograph—in our morning newspapers, in our social-media feeds, on our computer screens next to advertisements for diamond watches or cruises or yoga pants. And many of us fear that we don't know how to

look at them, or what to do in response to what we see. We feel helpless. Useless. And then we feel ashamed. Better not to look at all. Better to avoid images of the dead.[2]

And then there's imaginary death. Think about the body count in Marvel movies like *Avengers: Endgame*. A building burns on screen as we sip a Coke; the camera pans to a bloody fistfight as we munch on a fistful of popcorn. Through modern entertainment, we can witness more tragedy in an hour than most people experience in a lifetime, but we're detached from it. Witnessing a bomb detonate in real life might give people PTSD. Seeing the same thing on screen may make us tear up for a moment, but when the movie ends, we move on with our day, unfazed.

So how do we respond when death comes crashing back into our awareness? How will your teen handle news of school shootings, virus outbreaks, and opioid overdoses? This is the world your teen is navigating, and they need your guidance. When you and your teen courageously face the reality of death, you accept the invitation to focus on what really matters in life.

When you and your
teen courageously face
the reality of death, you
accept the invitation
to focus on what really
matters in life.

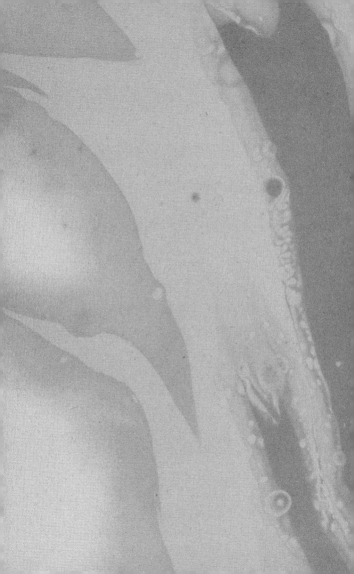

HOW SHOULD CHRISTIANS THINK ABOUT DEATH?

CHRISTIANS SERVE the One who has over-come death and the grave. This should fill us with a tremendous sense of awe and worshipful gratitude, but we can't get there until we truly reckon with what our Savior overcame. In a sermon series on the book of Ephesians, Martyn Lloyd-Jones put it like this:

> My dear friends, you and I don't realize what the power of God in us is because we've never quite realized the power of death. Read your Bible again and keep your eye on what it says about the power of death. Death is something that holds us, it binds us, it bends us, it chains us! There is nothing that so holds and grips and grasps as death.[3]

The Bible was not written by people whose lives were insulated from death. Israel lived through most of the Old Testament under the shadow of some oppressive empire. Death was the ever-present weapon, wielded against anyone who even thought about transgressing. The Romans' practice of crucifixion made those who were dying into warning signs, discouraging onlookers from daring to provoke their wrath.

It is against this historical backdrop that the apostle Paul wrote in 1 Corinthians 15:54-57:

> When the perishable has been
> clothed with the imperishable,
> and the mortal with immortality,
> then the saying that is written
> will come true: "Death has been
> swallowed up in victory."

"Where, O death, is your victory?
Where, O death, is your sting?"
The sting of death is sin, and the
power of sin is the law. But thanks
be to God! He gives us the victory
through our Lord Jesus Christ.

In short, we should regard death soberly,
but not with fear.

Christians serve the
One who has overcome
death and the grave.

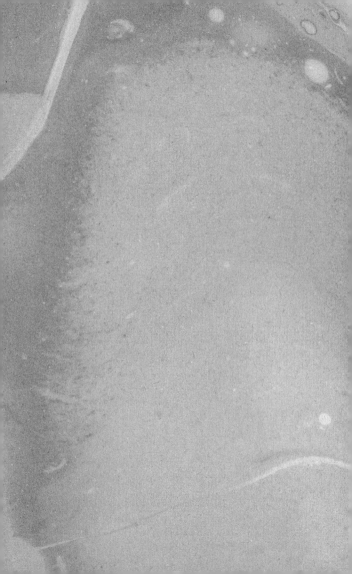

BUT WILL I TRAUMATIZE MY TEEN?

COUNTERINTUITIVELY, there's often more power (guilt/shame/fear) around the things that we don't talk about—the topics that are socially taboo—than the things we discuss openly. Here's how Joy Clarkson described her first Ash Wednesday service, literally centered on the statement "Remember you are dust and to dust you shall return":

> It was such a relief. To have someone say it out loud. To say it out loud with a hundred other people. Death, the unalterable fact of life, was acknowledged in the company of others; modern life's best kept secret was looked in the face. And as we all went forward, I no longer felt alone in this mystery. I was accompanied by a great cloud of witnesses before me. And most of all, I suddenly

knew I was accompanied by Jesus. The strange claim of my faith is that God made himself vulnerable to death.[4]

Paradoxically, Jesus defeated death by dying. "He humbled himself by becoming obedient to death—even death on a cross!" (Philippians 2:8). Death is a central theme of Christianity. When someone follows in the way of Jesus, their old, sinful self is crucified with Him, and God gives them new life. One day, physical death will give way to bodily resurrection, to a life that lasts forever. Death is the doorway to these important, necessary, and beautiful events.

If your teen thinks about death a lot or is fascinated by all the gory details of, say, Egyptian mummification, they're not abnormal or doing anything wrong.

While teens are infamous for their cavalier attitudes toward risk and danger, discussing death can encourage them toward a sober understanding of the impact of their choices, and even help them remember that they have a limited amount of time to exist.

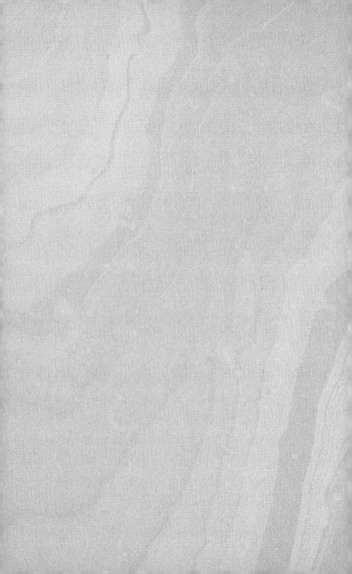

Lynnette Lounsbury, a high school writing teacher, explains,

> The problem with ignoring something, or brushing teenagers off by telling them not to be morbid, is that they become even more fascinated. . . . In the past, death was such a part of everyday life it was simply and frankly discussed, and in my opinion, our students crave opportunities to have candid discussions about their mortality. [5]

As you read the Bible, you'll find plenty of death (and even graphic violence) in its pages. So when Scripture encourages us to think about "whatever is true, whatever is noble, whatever is right, whatever is pure, whatever is lovely, whatever is admirable" (Philippians 4:8), Paul isn't saying we should ignore violence and pretend the world is prettier than it is. Death is a real part of our fallen world, and Ecclesiastes 7:2 insists that we "take this to heart."

So far from traumatizing our kids, talking about death can be a way to ground them in reality. While teens are infamous for their cavalier attitudes toward risk and danger, discussing death can encourage them toward a sober understanding of the impact of their choices, and even help them remember that they have a limited amount of time to exist.

HOW SHOULD I TALK TO MY TEEN ABOUT DEATH?

DEATH VISITS our communities in radically different ways. It can be expected or unexpected, natural or unnatural. Talking about the death of a person who lived to see their grandchildren grow up is utterly different from talking about a three-year-old dying in a car accident or a fifteen-year-old taking her own life. Yet every instance of death feels gruesome and strange, even though it's the one thing we can all be sure of. Simone de Beauvoir put it this way:

> There is no such thing as a natural death: nothing that happens to a man is ever natural, since his presence calls the world into question. All men must die: but for every man his death is an accident and, even if he knows it and consents to it, an unjustifiable violation.[6]

Whether your child has already lost someone or you're preemptively beginning this conversation, here are a few principles to keep in mind as you navigate your unique situation.

Be clear. It may seem kind to tell your child that someone has "passed away," but that phrase and others like it can be confusing. For instance, young children may become afraid to go to sleep if their loved one is described as "eternally asleep." Instead, use the words *dead* and *died*.

Be honest. Children should know the real cause of death so they don't invent reasons that might involve guilt or shame— for example, *My mom must've done something wrong*, or *I caused my aunt's death when I said such and such*. You don't have to explain every detail, but it's

Our kids are always evaluating whether we are safe people to express themselves with. How would we like to be responded to if we were in their shoes?

important to communicate how the person died.

Clarify. What did your child take away from what you told them? Do they have any questions about what happened? Does anything need to be explained further?

A note about pets: The loss of a pet is often a person's first exposure to death.[7] It's natural to grieve our pets, since they often become beloved family members. A friend of ours reminisced about her family's two Labs:

> For me, both Bristol and Piper were companions that could never turn on me, lose my trust, or disagree on what we were going to do. It sounds silly and extreme, but in a way, you have

to look at losing a pet like that as losing a confidant, someone or something that knows you and cannot judge you in the slightest.

Encourage your child to verbalize their feelings after they lose a pet. Rather than muscling through this loss or comparing the pet's death to the "real" hardships that other people face, let your child process the fact that their friend is gone. And that's hard.

Our kids are always evaluating whether we are safe people to express themselves with. How will we respond if they cry? If they lash out in anger? If they express sincere doubts and frustrations? How would we like to be responded to if we were in their shoes?

WHAT QUESTIONS DO TEENS HAVE ABOUT DEATH?

WHETHER A TEEN loses someone close to them or reads about an atrocity committed in another country, an encounter with death will often bring questions about God's character and the nature of reality rocketing to the surface. A world that once seemed beautiful and exciting can suddenly feel dark and overwhelming. Here are some of the questions your teen might be wrestling with:

- How could God let something like this happen?

- Why isn't every death quick and painless? Why does God allow some people to suffer before they die?

- How can I live in a world where things like this happen?

- How can I go on if I will never see this person again?

- Why are we alive if the whole point is to die and go to heaven someday?

- Does God really send people to hell after they die? Will my friend really be tortured forever for not believing in Jesus?

- What if I'm afraid of death? How can I not be afraid?

These questions are weighty. They are tied to traumas, fears, and hopes. Your teen needs you to tread lightly, to treat their objections and questions with respect, and to acknowledge that people have been wrestling with these questions since the dawn of time and that there aren't always satisfying answers.

Jewish culture recognizes that death brings very painful questions to the

Whether a teen loses someone close to them or reads about an atrocity committed in another country, an encounter with death will often bring questions about God's character and the nature of reality rocketing to the surface.

surface and that giving an answer isn't usually the point. The practice of sitting shiva is about being present with people who are grieving, especially for the first seven days after someone has died. Not offering words of advice or wisdom. Not trying to fix an unfixable situation. Allowing torrents of grief and moments of numbness to come and go without offering unhelpful statements like "You'll see them again in heaven" or "They're in a better place now." Being present is enough.

> Shiva is a time to . . . share memories and stories about the deceased. It's a time to honor a mourner's grief process without trying to correct or fix it, as the focus is on giving space to mourn without constraint. Your job as the visitor is to let mourners know

you are there as unconditional
support and presence.[8]

We're not saying that teens should avoid
tough theological questions. But after the
loss of someone they love, information
will probably fall flat.

WHY IS TALKING ABOUT DEATH SO HARD?

JULIAN OF NORWICH, a theologian of the four-teenth century, lived through six iterations of the black plague. Julian experienced these outbreaks over and over and over again. She had questions for God, born out of her torturous experience. "Where are you? Do you care what is happening to your world? If you knew what sin was going to do, why didn't you stop it? Why create us at all?"[9]

Perhaps we are afraid to talk about death because Julian's questions are also our questions. What was God thinking when He set the world in motion? Is all this pain worth it? Maybe you're afraid of adding to your teen's confusion, especially if you don't have clear answers or peace of mind about the people you've loved and lost. But more than clear-cut answers or easy theology, your teens need your honesty. They need your presence.

The medieval church realized that people needed a way to approach death; a way to air their fears of mortality and a painful end; guidance about what to say and do as they walked with their loved ones to the grave. Enter the *Ars moriendi*, the Art of Dying, which instructed Christians how to die well.[10] The church walked bravely into the spaces of deepest grief, fiercest pain, and most gut-wrenching sickness to offer practical help and the comfort that Christ is with us even in the worst of what existence brings. Our teens need their own *Ars moriendi*, even if it's complex and messy and incomplete. They have questions. Are we brave enough to listen? To face death for ourselves so that we can lead them well?

More than clear-cut answers or easy theology, your teens need your honesty. They need your presence.

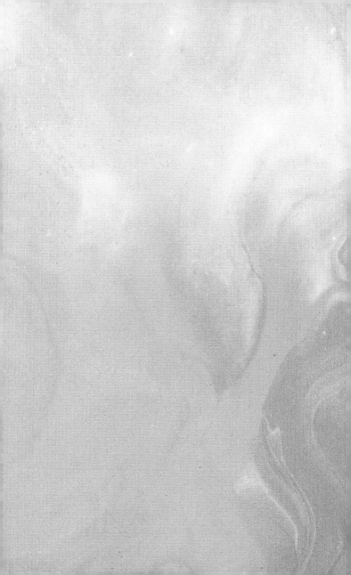

HOW DOES THE DEATH OF A LOVED ONE IMPACT A TEEN?

IT WOULD BE EASIER to deal with death if the grieving process were the same for everyone. Five simple steps to work through. A clear finish line. Relief. Peace. But as we know, everyone's journey through grief is different. And a teen's process through grief is impacted by many factors:

- What kind of social support system do they have?

- What were the circumstances of the death?

- Did they unexpectedly find the body?

- What was their relationship with the person who died?

- To what extent were they involved in the dying process?

- What is their age and maturity level?

- Do they have any previous experience with death?[11]

While grief is different for everyone, here are some common reactions to prepare for:

Buried emotions: Teens grieve deeply but often work very hard to hide their feelings. Fearing the vulnerability that comes with expression, they look for distractions rather than staying with the grief process long enough to find real relief. Their feelings may appear to quickly turn on and off, much like flipping a light switch. Teens can act as if nothing has happened while they are breaking up inside.

Concern for you: If you are grieving the death of someone you love, your kids are concerned about you even as they're figuring out how to handle their own emotions.

Guilt: Teens may experience guilt about something they should have done differently or about an argument with the person who died. Really, they're asking, *Did I somehow cause this person I love to die? Maybe they wouldn't be dead if I had done this, said this, or avoided this.* Reassure them that those thoughts are normal, and remind them that they aren't actually responsible.

Anger: "Children often express anger about the death. They may focus on someone they feel is responsible. They may feel angry at God. They may feel angry at the person who died for leaving them. Family members sometimes become the focus of this anger, because they are near and are 'safe' targets."

Risky behavior: "Older children and teens may . . . drive recklessly, get into fights, drink alcohol, smoke cigarettes, or use drugs. They may become involved in sexual activity or delinquency. They may start to have problems at school or conflicts with friends."

Fear: Your teen may be afraid that they'll forget the person and feel guilty about even having that fear (*If this person means so much to me, how could I possibly forget about them?*).

Teens grieve deeply
but often work very hard
to hide their feelings.

Be ready—for tears. Angry outbursts. Confusion. Silence. Numbness. Sarcastic comments. Slammed doors. If you're concerned about your teen's health, the article "The Grieving Teen" by Helen Fitzgerald and the booklet "After a Loved One Dies—How Children Grieve" by David Schonfeld and Marcia Quackenbush (quoted in the previous list) can help you identify behaviors that indicate unhealthy coping and are signs to get professional help.[12]

WHAT IF DEATH SEEMS APPEALING TO MY TEEN?

TALKING ABOUT DEATH as an abstract concept is fine, but what if our teens are fascinated by dying? What if they are experiencing so much pain that they just want to be done with it all?

> It is an odd and frightening sensation to wish you were dead. After my husband died I fervently wished I could die, too. The first time I read that grieving people sometimes fantasize about death, I was relieved. My entire life I had appreciated the gift of life; to suddenly and frequently wish it away was a disconcerting and lonely experience.
>
> **MICHELE HERNANDEZ**[13]

Relief: from endless homework, stress at home, trauma, bullying, self-consciousness, constant social anxiety . . . Sometimes, especially after a friend or family member dies, death can seem like the only way to get away from a life that's falling apart or emotions that don't make sense. Some teens may begin to contemplate suicide as an escape route.

It's important to understand the difference between passive and active suicidal ideation. Passive suicidal ideation sounds like "I wish I could take a long nap and never wake up." Active suicidal ideation means that someone has a plan in place for taking their life. It can be the next step for someone experiencing passive suicidal ideation, especially if they continue to feel hopeless and overwhelmed.

If you even suspect that your child is struggling with any form of suicidal ideation, stop reading this guide and immediately seek help. Contact your family physician and tell them your teen is at risk of suicide and must be seen immediately. If a doctor cannot see them right away for whatever reason, do not leave your child alone until they can be seen and evaluated by a health-care professional qualified to assess adolescent behavioral health. If necessary, take your child to the nearest emergency room or urgent care center, demand priority, and do not leave the physician's office until next steps are in place (such as referral to a specialist, assessments, evaluations, treatment plans, outpatient/inpatient programs, etc.).

If you even suspect that your child is struggling with any form of suicidal ideation, stop reading this guide and immediately seek help.

WHAT DOES MY TEEN NEED?

AS YOU LISTEN for the Holy Spirit's invitation, think about how your teen might experience God's love through your presence in their life. Here are some initial ideas:

Comfort and attention. We want our community to notice our pain. Your teen will want their friends to text them, to ask if they're doing okay. This isn't selfish. We encourage you to say that this desire for support is normal and good.

Consistent check-ins. If it's helpful, set a reminder on your phone to check in weekly at first (through a text, call, or time together), then every few weeks, and then monthly. Especially as time passes, people will forget that your teen is still grieving.

Space to process. Your teen may not have the words to explain how they're doing, but they still want to be asked if they're okay. Give them space to process when they're ready. But don't be offended and/or freak out if they don't know how to answer your questions.

Time together. Do some activities that don't require intense processing. Watch a show, drive around and get your errands done, hike, play basketball (or whatever sport your teen enjoys), feed some ducks, get your nails done, play a video game, etc.

Permission to let go. Here's a question to ask your teen when you feel they're ready: "Now that this person is gone, do you have a hole that needs filling?" Was the person who died a friend, mentor, or adventure buddy? It's okay to have another best friend, even though it's perfectly normal to feel guilty about replacing

As you listen for the
Holy Spirit's invitation,
think about how your
teen might experience
God's love through your
presence in their life.

someone. Your teen will probably want to talk through their emotions and fears surrounding "moving on," including whether it's bad, what it looks like, etc.

Opportunities to remember. We recently heard a story about Trey and his family. On the day his grandmother passed away, they went to the store, bought some cookies & cream ice cream, and ate it after dinner as a way of remembering and honoring her. (You guessed it—she loved cookies & cream.)

Community helps us remember those we've lost, through stories, photos, and conversation. By simply saying, "Wow, Granddad would've loved looking at these flowers with us" or "Being at this restaurant makes me miss your mom. This was her favorite place to eat," you're modeling healthy grief in small but important ways.

And you're giving your teen a glimpse of your internal world.

Good questions about the person who died. Ask your teen, "What's something you admired about ____ that you hope to emulate?" "Did they have a hobby that you want to try out?"

Counseling. Inviting a professional to help your teen process their grief has nothing to do with your ability as a parent. You're not losing your importance; you're simply giving your teen every possible outlet for figuring things out and pursuing healing. A friend of ours explains,

> A friend I really cared about died my freshman year of high school in a tornado. I remember calling my mom as soon as I got home from school, and she dropped

67

everything and came straight home, which was critical. What I think I needed afterward, and what probably never occurred to her, was months of serious grief counseling. My parents were there for me, certainly. I wasn't isolated. But I had no tools to process the experience.

Help thinking through what to say. Another friend of ours lost her sister unexpectedly about eighteen months ago, and she's noticed that innocent get-to-know-you conversations can become uncomfortable when someone asks if she has siblings. Should she say that she only has three because her sister is dead? What if she says that she has four siblings and then someone asks, "Oh, where do they live?" Long pause. "Well . . . my sister is dead. But the rest of them live here, here, and here." Yikes. Now she's managing a stranger's awkwardness, and her own peace with her sister's death is called into question anytime she has this weirdly vulnerable interaction.

Our friend found it really helpful to talk with her parents about how they handled interactions like that, and she was encouraged that they didn't always know how to respond either.

Be gracious with yourself. Processing your own grief while watching out for your child is so difficult. Give yourself lots of grace in this process.

WHAT IF I DON'T KNOW WHAT TO SAY?

ONE OF THE MOST humbling and striking examples of grief is found in John 11. Jesus' close friends Mary and Martha are mourning the death of their brother Lazarus. It's a rough story. They sent word to Jesus, begging Him to come to their town to heal Lazarus. But Jesus waited . . . days. When He finally arrived, Mary accused Him, "Lord, if you had been here, my brother would not have died" (John 11:32). They were blunt. Angry. Confused. They must have felt abandoned and betrayed. Jesus would heal strangers, but not His own friend? Surprisingly, Jesus didn't defend Himself or explain His reasoning. He didn't tell them to have more faith or to be less emotional. Instead, He cried (see John 11:35). He joined them in their pain, even though He knew He was about to raise Lazarus from the dead, which was

His plan all along. But He also knew that the hope of eventual resurrection didn't change Mary's and Martha's feelings in the moment. Instead of insisting that they change, Jesus joined them there.

Even though we view death as part of God's larger story and know He will restore and renew all things, there is room in Christianity for real anguish, confusion, and even anger. The Psalms are full of lamentation. God isn't asking us to have more appropriate emotional responses to death. God's response in Jesus was to grieve with His friends. Can you offer this type of support to your teen in their questions and in their pain? Are you willing to grieve with them instead of trying to fix or deemphasize when death inevitably touches someone they care about?

Even though we view
death as part of God's larger
story and know He will
restore and renew all things,
there is room in Christianity
for real anguish, confusion,
and even anger.

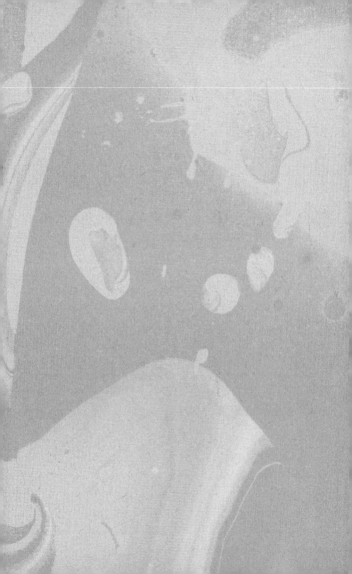

Most of us just want and need to be listened to. Your teen isn't looking for a sermon. They want a hug, a good cry, and an "I'm sorry. That sucks." Exhale. You don't need to have all the answers.

This is uncomfortable, and we don't have to make it comfortable. Perhaps the best thing you can do is to be there with them. You are in this together. And Christ is with you as well.

REFLECTION QUESTIONS

1. As I imagine talking with my teen about death, what emotions rise to the surface?

2. What was my first experience with death?

3. What has my experience with grief been like? Are there any losses in my life that I haven't fully processed?

4. When someone I love dies, what is my natural first response? What coping mechanisms do I gravitate toward, whether healthy or unhealthy?

5. How did my parents or caretakers respond to and talk about death? What did they do well? What do I want to do differently with my own teen?

DISCUSSION QUESTIONS

1. Are you afraid to talk about death? Why or why not?

2. What legacy do you hope to leave for the people who come after you? What legacies have been left for you by older relatives and mentors?

3. What does culture teach us about death? What are the pros and cons of these messages?

QUESTIONS TO ASK WHEN A DEATH HAPPENS IN YOUR TEEN'S COMMUNITY

1. How can we support the people who loved this person?

2. Practically, what will it look like to show up for them this week, six months from now, and three years from now?

QUESTIONS TO ASK WHEN YOUR TEEN LOSES SOMEONE CLOSE TO THEM

1. In the midst of this loss, what are you feeling that you didn't expect to feel?

2. In the midst of this loss, what would be most comforting for you?

3. What can it look like to celebrate this person's life and continue to remember them?

4. What qualities did you love about this person? Are there any ways that you hope to be more like them?

ADDITIONAL RESOURCES

- The Order of the Good Death, https://www.orderofthegooddeath.com/

- The Art of Dying Well, https://www.artofdyingwell.org/

- GriefShare, https://www.griefshare.org

VIDEOS

- Ask a Mortician, "Overcoming Death Denial in Your Family," https://www.youtube.com/watch?v=0WOyFErcTHU

- Ask a Mortician, "Talk to Your Children about Death," https://www.youtube.com/watch?v=0gUOP9IvZew

- Ask a Mortician, "Confronting Your Death," https://www.youtube.com/watch?v=CN7ZD9uw7LQ

ARTICLES AND BOOKS

- Helen Fitzgerald, "The Grieving Teen," American Hospice Foundation, https://americanhospice.org/grieving-children/someone-you-love-has-died-a-book-for-grieving-children/

- Cassie Barthuly, "10 Popular Jewish Funeral Prayers and Poems," Cake, https://www.joincake.com/blog/jewish-funeral-prayers/

- "Grief," TeensHealth, https://kidshealth.org/en/teens/someone-died.html

- "Ars Moriendi," The Art of Dying Well, http://www.artofdyingwell.org/about-this-site/ars-moriendi/

- "Coping with Losing a Pet," HelpGuide, https://www.helpguide.org/articles/grief/coping-with-losing-a-pet.htm

- Guy Winch, "Why We Need to Take Pet Loss Seriously," *Scientific American*, https://www.scientificamerican.com/article/why-we-need-to-take-pet-loss-seriously/

- Carolyn Bunge, "Tips for Offering Condolences," Cake, https://www.joincake.com/blog/how-to-offer-condolences/

- Lisa Milbrand, "How to Explain Death to a Child, A Step-by-Step Guide," Parents, https://www.parents.com/toddlers

-preschoolers/development/social
/talking-to-kids-about-death/

- Cory Turner, "The Dog Isn't Sleeping: How to Talk with Children about Death," NPR, https://www.npr.org/2019/03
/04/698309351/the-dog-isnt-sleeping
-how-to-talk-with-children-about-death

- "Talking to Adolescents about Death," Lakeview Middle School, https://www
.greenville.k12.sc.us/lakeview/Upload
/uploads/Parent%20Guide.pdf

- Deborah Serani, "The Do's and Don'ts of Talking with a Child about Death," Psychology Today, https://www
.psychologytoday.com/us/blog/two
-takes-depression/201612/the-dos-and
-donts-talking-child-about-death

- Lynnette Young, "Young People Are Dying to Talk about Death," The Guardian, https://www.theguardian.com
/commentisfree/2014/jun/08/young
-people-are-dying-to-talk-about-death

- The Great Divorce, A Grief Observed, and The Problem of Pain by C. S. Lewis

- *On Death* by Timothy Keller

- *Being Mortal* by Atul Gawande

AUDIO

- "We're All Going to Die," *Speaking with Joy* podcast, https://joyclarkson.com /home/2018/2/12/remember-you-have -to-die

- "Mimi Dixon—Julian of Norwich," *Renovaré Podcast*, https://renovare.org /podcast/episode-95-mimi-dixon-julian -of-norwich

- "Hell and Heaven," *Ask NT Wright Anything* podcast, https://podcasts.apple .com/us/podcast/18-hell-and-heaven /id1441656192?i=1000444756779

- "DUST," Kings Kaleidoscope, https://www .youtube.com/watch?v=F0_uROWStpc

- "Centering Prayer," The Liturgists, https://www.youtube.com/watch?v =brwjlIpNSug

- "Vapor,"The Liturgists, https://www .youtube.com/watch?v=fOH6qYTOo0c

RECAP

- This is a difficult topic. Thank you for choosing to walk with your teen through personal grief and loss, or for preparing them to encounter death in the future.

- Western society is structured to keep us from thinking about death. Teens encounter death through media and entertainment, but often these glimpses of death are gory or fantastical. They need honest conversations about mortality to begin grappling with their own limitations.

- Christians have a nuanced understanding of death. Christ conquered death—yet death is terrible. We don't have to be afraid of dying— yet some of our deepest pain comes from encountering death.

- Teens have tough questions about death. Be willing to really listen to them.

- Spend time with your teen. Be with them. Even if you don't have answers (actually, the fewer answers and clichés, the better). Even when it feels uncomfortable. Even when your heart is breaking. Your presence is enough.

NOTES

1. Erika Hayasaki, "Death Is Having a Moment," *Atlantic*, October 25, 2013, https://www.theatlantic.com/health/archive/2013/10/death-is-having-a-moment/280777/.

2. Sarah Sentilles, "When We See Photographs of Some Dead Bodies and Not Others," *New York Times Magazine*, August 14, 2018, https://www.nytimes.com/2018/08/14/magazine/media-bodies-censorship.html.

3. Martyn Lloyd-Jones, "Power to Us-ward Who Believe," YouTube, video, 44:04, https://www.youtube.com/watch?v=LK9ykyvrnMM.

4. Joy Marie Clarkson, "We're All Going to Die," February 13, 2018, https://joyclarkson.com/home/2018/2/12/remember-you-have-to-die.

5. Lynnette Lounsbury, "Young People Are Dying to Talk about Death," *Guardian*, June 7, 2014, https://www.theguardian.com/commentisfree/2014/jun/08/young-people-are-dying-to-talk-about-death.

6. Simone de Beauvoir, *A Very Easy Death* (New York: Knopf Doubleday, 1985), 106.

7. Lawrence Robinson, Jeanne Segal, and Robert Segal, "Coping with Losing a Pet," HelpGuide, December 5, 2022, https://www.helpguide.org/articles/grief/coping-with-losing-a-pet.htm.

8. Erin Coriell, "Sitting Shiva for Non-Jews: Etiquette & What Happens," Cake, August 20, 2022, https://www.joincake.com/blog/sitting-shiva/.

9. Miriam Dixon and Nathan Foster, "Mimi Dixon—Julian of Norwich," in *Renovaré, podcast, 57:15, September 3, 2017,* https://renovare.org/podcast/episode-95-mimi-dixon-julian-of-norwich.

10. Simon Thomas, "Ars Moriendi—The Art of Dying," Polonsky Foundation Digitization Project, accessed January 30, 2023, http://bav.bodleian.ox.ac.uk/news/ars-moriendi-the-art-of-dying.

11. "How to Help a Grieving Teen," Dougy Center, November 12, 2020, https://www.dougy.org /resource-articles/how-to-help-a-grieving -teen.

12. Helen Fitzgerald, "The Grieving Teen," American Hospice Foundation, 2000, https:// americanhospice.org/grieving-children /someone-you-love-has-died-a-book-for -grieving-children/; David J. Schonfeld and Marcia Quackenbush, "After a Loved One Dies—How Children Grieve," New York Life Foundation, 2009, https://portal.ct.gov /-/media/DCF/Prevention/PDF/AfteraLoved OneDiesHowChildrenGrievepdf.pdf.

13. Michele Hernandez, "My Death Wish," TAPS, September 21, 2009, https://www.taps.org /articles/15-4/deathwish.

PARENT GUIDES TO SOCIAL MEDIA
BY AXIS

It's common to feel lost in your teen's world. Let these be your go-to guides on social media, how it affects your teen, and how to begin an ongoing conversation about faith that matters.

BUNDLE THESE 5 BOOKS AND SAVE